Heal With Me

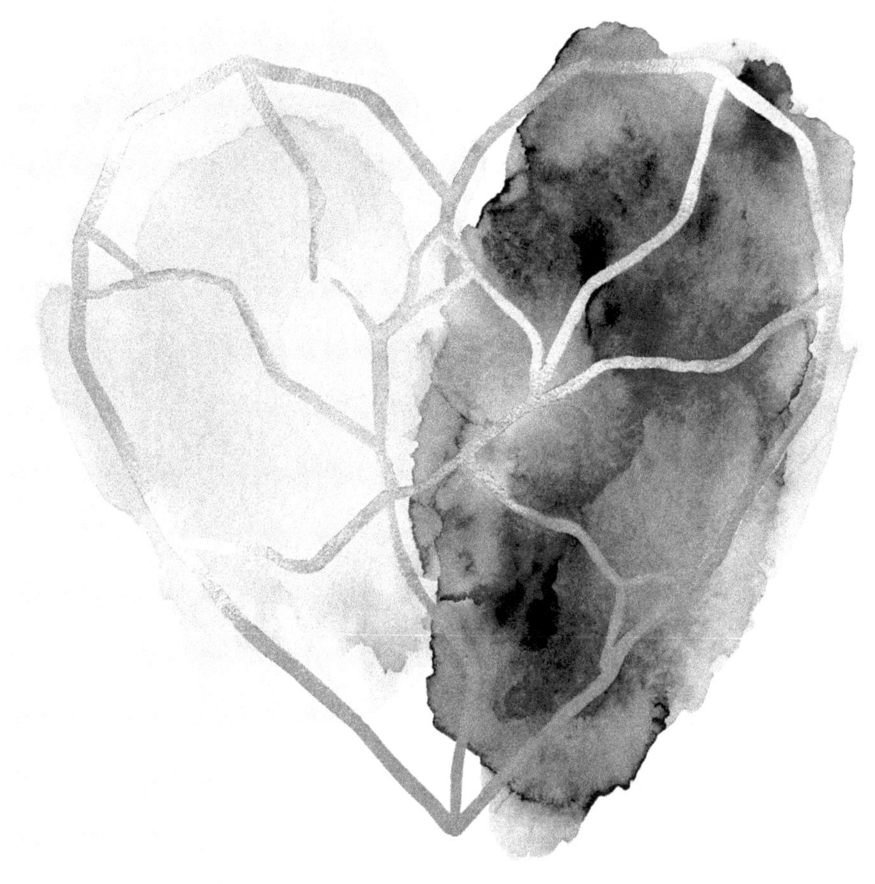

HEAL WITH ME

A roadmap through the beautiful mess of becoming whole

Dr. Ronda Wallace

ISBN: 979-8-218-89898-4

Cover design by: Alisha Phipps

Book design by: Carolyn Vaughan (carolyn.j.vaughan@gmail.com)

Dedication

This book is dedicated to literally everyone but especially to My Mommy, Sandra Renise Scales-Lambert who has never left my side and to my Daddy, Maurice V. Wallace Sr. who gave me the best advice ever, "Let it go!"

A special dedication to My Big Lionel, Lionel Lambert Sr, My Granny, Sabra Leah Watt-Ward and My Granny Girl, Doreatha Wallace. You are truly missed.
I finally finished!

To my SisterCousin, Nikole, you have no idea of how much you have inspired me my entire life!

Meacham Park — stand up! All of you have supported me non-stop! Love y'all a long time!

To my editor, Kim. I was sent to you with intention. You then became exactly who I needed. Love you, Chica.

To The Fab Four. Four reasons why I go hard!
Mommy loves you!

Foreword

Ronda, Peaches, roRo, H.M. —

I don't even know where to begin.

Ever since I can remember, I've always looked up to you. You've been the sister I never had. From the times we played "house" and I always wanted you to be my mom, or when we played school and I insisted on you being the teacher — it was always because, even back then, you embodied what it meant to be strong, dedicated, and organized. You carried yourself like an adult, even when we were just kids.

Now, fast forward forty years, and you are still that person — only more. You bring those same qualities to every role you hold; as a mother, an educator, sister, daughter, and a friend. I am so incredibly proud of the woman that you are.

You and I have done this thing called life together. If people only knew the stories we could tell. Through every high and every low, we've stood side by side. We've been each other's biggest cheerleaders, and I am honored that you chose me to write this foreword.

Writing this book is an amazing accomplishment. I applaud your willingness to be vulnerable and honor your tenacity to keep going, even in the moments when giving up might have felt easier. Your story—your truth—is powerful, and I have no doubt it will touch and transform the lives of those who read it.

You are brave. You are honest. You are a light.

To the reader: As you open this book, prepare yourself to laugh, cry, reflect, and grow. This book is more than a story — it's a testimony. And if you let it—it just might change your life, too.

With all my love and admiration,
Your Sister
Nikole "Nikki" H.M.

Preface

This life that I am living is not for the weak! Chile. Some things I just don't understand and other shit I just had to learn to let go because I am too big and too old to try to figure it out. To my amazement, at this current lovely age; I have overcome some real challenges — and did it with positive energy. I have been writing this book for years. There are at least five notebooks and a couple of Google Doc pages with My Book written at the top. Why do we play with God when He directly tells us to do something? In the mighty words of every black momma, "You gon' learn today."

The last seven years have been extremely tough for me. I use the word tough because of enduring so much hardship and pain; I had to withstand many adversities and challenges. I questioned my career choice, faced challenges with my children and for the first time in my adult life — I understood the value of life and reality of death. I am still standing, although two of my Grannies have transitioned to Heaven within a month apart. Whew! That understanding piece was detrimental to my healing. Still.

I often reflect and ask myself, "How the hell did I get through that?" or "Thank you God for bringing me through that!" Words that resonated with me daily. I never knew how strong I was until I left a narcissist relationship that literally drained the life out of me. I later made the hard decision to challenge myself as an Instructional Leader in a very different capacity. See, people don't know what you go through; or better yet — allow themselves to know/see your daily challenges. I will talk about that "allow" word later because I was "today" years old when I figured out that I was "allowing" shit to go down in my life. Yep. Sounds stupid, huh. We really just live our lives as we know how and do dumb shit along the way. That's the "allow." The dumb shit.

Y'all! I am so grateful for all the challenges that I have gone through because the end is going to be mind-blowing. Writing this book is my therapy and you will understand better as you begin to read the shenanigans and foolishness behind the thoughts of a Principalchick. And look, I coined Principalchick about twenty years ago when God first told me to start writing. It was created as my "alias" in education. Now, I am here. The Black Carrie Bradshaw. Your Principalchick for life!

My prayer is that I inspire, encourage and provoke thought as you heal from the challenges that you are enduring. Hold on tight because there's a bit of everything in this book. These are my crazy chronicles!

Heal with me.

XOXO,

Your Principalchick

Table of Contents

Chapter One: Real Talk —The Black Carrie Bradshaw. . . . 11
Chapter Two: Purpose. 15
Chapter Three: The Switch Up. 19
Chapter Four: Winning While Losing 23
Chapter Five: My Greatest Obsession. 25
Chapter Six: Becoming Roni. 29
Chapter Seven: Just Around Here Allowing 31
Chapter Eight: It's Always Your Own Kids. 33
Chapter Nine: The Professional Chick. 37
Chapter Ten: The Unstoppable Chick. 41
Chapter Eleven: The Praying Chick. 45
Chapter Twelve: Dealing with Trauma. 49
Chapter Thirteen: Who Told Me to Be a Parent?. 53
Chapter Fourteen: Can't Make This Up. 57
Chapter Fifteen: Shower Cry. 61
Chapter Sixteen: When You Are Not Good. 65
Chapter Seventeen: The Other Side of Healing. 67
Chapter Eighteen: The Heal With Me Commandments. 69
Chapter Nineteen: Turn Your Pain Into Purpose. 73
Chapter Twenty: Finally...I Have Arrived!. 75
About the Author. 79

Chapter One

Real Talk — The Black Carrie Bradshaw

And so it begins. All the thoughts and questions, because I am trying to make sense of foolishness. Is that a thing? Making sense of foolishness and/or foolish behavior? Why do we make excuses for FB (foolish behavior) and why do we follow up with shenanigans? What am I talking about? Life. We wonder why "stuff" happens to us. Because simply put—we allow it. Yep, hard lesson for me too. Stop frowning your face up. Because you do it too; just allow freestyling in your lives for every reason or use every excuse that you can think of:

I just need to keep the peace.

I'm not dealing with this today.

I will work on it later.

I'm too busy.

He/she/they will get better.

It will be ok.

Go with the flow.

Miss the flow.

On the flo'.

Ignore.

This is us all day long with our dysfunctional thoughts. Then we wonder why we have a headache. Freestyling is not having a plan. That's it. We try to go on day by day without a plan, entertaining folk that we don't want or need to entertain, spending money and going to work because it's routine. In the meantime, we're creating bad patterns. It's not intentional, but that's what we do. We keep it going when we need to let it go. We want to see what happens because we are natural hardheaded beings. Head just as hard. We are just reading the Bible, burning sage, asking for anyone to pray for us, lying on Facebook, dating whoever and two stepping into our negative routine that we created—and have the nerve to be frustrated. *Side note: stop burning that sage.*

We created our own frustration by allowing things that we know are wrong to continue in our lives; we executed our own FB (foolish behavior).

Now, it's habitual. Why? It's all learned. We emulated someone in our family at some point in our lives—and just ran with it.

Now we're just running without destination or purpose. We often stop and pause, but love putting on those running shoes. What are we running from or to? One word, life. I call myself the Black Carrie Bradshaw because I understood, and at some point could relate to every thought that this fictional character had on the hit tv show *Sex in the City*. Carrie Bradshaw was a fictional fashionista, played by actress Sarah Jessica Parker. She often wondered "why" and wanted to know how different life scenarios would play out as she justified some of her behaviors in her head. I do this all day long. My thoughts take over and then here comes those damn wonderings, and then I start asking myself questions, eventually writing them down after slipping into bed.

Side note, why am I not a blogger?

Ok, so when the thoughts over take my head, I tend to overthink. Overthinking is so overrated. Why do we talk ourselves into believing things that are non-existent (or maybe they are)? Like Carrie Bradshaw, I always leave a question lingering in my head until I stumble across the answer or the answer that "I" want. We do that too, don't we? Then we rely on our friends via brunch conversations to justify or debate the lingering question(s). Where am I going with this? To a place that will provoke us, ok me, to stop running. Running with thoughts and questions that we want the answers to; but really don't want the answers to, right? This goes back to the foolishness that I spoke about. The foolishness of believing that we can just continue running without a confirmed destination or purpose. We often run and pass by all the places that we need to stop and heal from. We are just running out of fear. Oh, that's me. Is it really just me or can you relate? We forget about purpose don't we? What is "*purpose*" and what does it mean?

Journal Entry

What are you running from?
Where are you running to?

Chapter Two

Purpose

Look, I am scared as hell of the word: purpose. I don't know why that word shakes me. So this is me researching the word, after my friend scolded me saying that I am not walking in my purpose. Honey, what am I doing then? Running? Yep. That's it. Ok, so back to it. This is me literally researching the word:

I read this definition first. *Purpose: something set up as an object or end to be attained: intention, resolution, determination.* Those three words had my attention. Then I read this one: *A subject under discussion or an action in the course of execution.* Whew chile! I started rocking back and forth and biting my nails. So, then I read this: *Have as one's intention or objective.* The example was: "*God has allowed suffering, even purposed it.*" I sat up straight. Stay with me because I am about to testify. I was then hit with the phrases:

On purpose — intentionally

To no purpose — with no result or effect; pointless

To the purpose — relevant or useful

I stood up and I shouted! Thank you God for the clarity! Thank you Friend, for gut punching me while we were deep in conversation and prayer! 'Cause wait, won't He give you clarity in the midst of confusion? I then went to my Bible: "*God wants to give you purpose. HE wants to bestow divine wisdom on you.*" *It's not that God is holding out on you to make you miserable. He desires you to have a joyful, ambitious, purposeful life.* I felt like I hit the jackpot, and did!

Running is suffering. Not being intentional is suffering. No resolution is suffering. Not being useful is suffering. No determination is suffering. "*God has allowed suffering, even purposed it.*" Did you read that correctly?

We are in our own way! Ok, I am in my own way! I just told y'all that God gave me a vision 15 years ago and I have just been ignoring His directive and freestyling; which led to my suffering BUT brought light to my purpose! It took my friend saying bluntly to me, "Girl, Principalchick should have blown up a long time ago. You are not walking in your purpose." God will remind us of our purpose even through others. I'm learning and I was taught something that day.

The day that I had the conversation with my friend, I was in a deep dark place. I didn't want to talk to anyone, but God said call her and I did. She listened, I cried, we talked about everything. I was not in a good place. She shared things with me that I know were very challenging to share as did I. That day felt intentional. The call was on purpose. While in my dark stage, I needed a beam of light and she was just that. Her anointing seeped through the phone and touched my spirit. It was intentional. She scolded me with love and admiration. She also checked me. Tuh! Confirmation: God knows what you need and who you need it from. My friend and I don't talk often, but when we do it is always a conversation that needs to happen. She is as real as it gets. Real talk. I now know my purpose. The struggle was real.

Let me take this first step in:

P — putting ME first!

U — understanding that I AM Amazing!

R — Reaching newness!

P — Praising God!

O — organizing my life!

S — staying away from unhealthy relationships!

E — establishing lifelong success!

THIS! Ha! Let me keep stepping!

Journal Entry

What does purpose mean to you?
Describe a time when you were gut punched.

Chapter Three

The Switch Up

I've been pleasing people my entire life. I wanted to make my parents proud of me and I needed to set an example for my siblings. I worked my butt off in college and then went back twice. I wanted to show my siblings that they could do anything and be whoever they wanted to be. After I had Kharynton, it was all about providing a better life for her. I did everything in my power to ensure that she had everything she needed and wanted; because I was the statistical unwed mother with an ex-partner that played no part in my child's life. Oh, I'm lying—he did that one time.

I often wonder what I would have become or done differently, had I not been set on pleasing those around me. I remember after giving birth to Kharynton, my daddy said, "No more baby showers before a bridal shower." Whew! I felt pressured and even after saying no to many proposals, I finally—reluctantly said, "yes." The reluctance was about truly not knowing the person that I was dating. We had only known each other for a year, and something in me knew that we were not on the same page. I was motivated by my career and had goals that I wanted to reach. He was a hustler surrounded by many female friends that stroked his ego. He fooled everyone with his personality. He was content. I was focused and determined. I vividly remember his aunt and grandma telling me not to marry him while we were dating. But, I couldn't help but to remember what my daddy told me with intention. Although I questioned myself the entire time, I got married and the rest is history. Divorced after 5 years. Two pregnancies, three kids and my first born. Single parent with an ex that switched up. Narcissist.

It wasn't just the switch up, it was the lies and the deceit. It was the family being accusatory even when I tried to stay neutral. It was his mom switching up when I told her the truth. The truth about his arrogance. The truth about his mental state. The truth about his anger that he couldn't manage. The truth about his treatment of my daughter. The truth about his female friends that were just email buddies. The truth about his truth. Yes. His truth. Chile, his truth was far and in between. But I kept calm and made decisions to better support my babies because I was a single parent while married.

The manipulation is where it started. And continued. The moments of being afraid to even talk. The moments of blaming myself. The moments of silence that broke my spirit. The moments of consistent prayer. It wasn't the fear of being a single parent—because remember I was already playing that role—it was the invested effort to make my life miserable by ripping apart my name and playing victim—to capacity. Again, the switch up.

Journal Entry

Describe a time when you felt that someone switched up on you. Explain how that made you feel.

Chapter Four

Winning While Losing

As a single parent, we often believe that the harder we work, the greater the pay off, right? We believe that we must take on all responsibilities from the absent parent, right? We challenge ourselves with working hard because we believe that working hard is what it takes, right? We fear being judged as an unwed mother or divorcee with a mysterious and rumor filled past, right? We convince ourselves that we are stronger than we truly are, right? We talk tough, right? We have something to prove because it's just me, myself and I, right? We overcompensate with our kids because we don't want them to feel abandoned or feel anything negative related to not being with their dad, right? We overlook things that we need to address out of fear, right? Whew! That word fear will have us in a chokehold. Won't it?

We make miracles happen in the lives of our children because we are protective. Protective. Protected. We are so confused because we are surviving instead of living. We are surviving the day to day antics of being a single parent out of fear. Fear of being judged. Fear of being looked upon as a bad mother. Fear of disappointing our kids. Fear of failing. Failure. So we put our all, everything, and ALL into bettering ourselves by working hard. A career and a job. A career and a job and back to school. A career, a job, back to school and yet another job. We do this. Right? We think that we are winning because we are doing all the things that will refrain from disappointing our kids, pleasing our parents and winning. Winning while we are losing. Losing. Losing our way. Losing our time. Losing our mind. But, I have graduated. Four times. A win. Right? I have moved up in my career. Four times. A win. Right? I have won awards. Four times. A win. Right? I can provide for my kids. All the time. Right?

All these wins, and yet I was losing. Losing myself. Losing my capacity. Losing my time. Losing my ability to breath without choking. Losing my faith. Losing. Losing my mind. Losing everything but this weight!

Journal Entry

What does winning — while losing mean to you? Give yourself an example.

Chapter Five

My Greatest Obsession

Anyone that knows me, knows that I have been overweight my entire life. It was my biggest struggle. I hated it when I received half compliments like,

"You have a pretty face," or "You have the best personality." I was always the big girl of my group of friends and cousins. I was ashamed. My- Entire- Life. I was ashamed of the comments made by everyone, including my own family. When I got to college I became the girl with the "tig ole' bitties." Yes, that statement triggered me each time it flowed from someone's mouth. I laughed because that's what big girls do right? We laugh it off as if the pain isn't bothering us or cutting through us. I was so good at it. I was the best leading actress as I was demeaned. Well, my breast reduction surgery gave me an opportunity to gain a little confidence because I could buy the bras from Victoria's Secret instead of Sears and/or JCPenney. You know, the white, beige and black granny bra selection? My whole life. Laughing. Though I stated that jokingly, I was traumatized each time it was time to go buy bras; funny how such a small thing could cause that much trauma. Why the hell were my breasts bigger than everyone else's?

I was so sad inside, but my vivid personality and socialite status allowed me to keep it pushing. Socialite status? Let me explain before y'all start talking mess. In high school, my shyness was my protector; in college being more vocal became my therapy. So when I state "socialite status" I am speaking of my choices to make plans every day and being around people. That became a part of my therapy. Letting people see who I am as a person, so that no one is focusing on my body size. Everyone has a cute chubby girl/ guy in their friend group, right?

I may be all over the place but pay close attention because I am not talking in a direct timeline. I am the one who believes that your weight has everything to do with everything, not limited to getting the "hot" guy or the career move that you have been waiting on. So, at some point, I began focusing on really losing weight. I waited forever just to get an appointment at the weight and wellness center that insurance takes. However, the journey began, and the weight was lost. I had so many people ask how I lost weight and to give them recipes. I am not and was not a good resource, so I would answer questions the best that I could as I was truly new to my weight loss and really did pray the weight off. Kidding but serious. If you know, you know.

Now, let me tell the other truth. As I prayed the weight off, I found myself interested in weight loss surgery. How embarrassing, right? Yep. I was completely embarrassed of even the thought. However, I entertained my thoughts, and made the call. Whew, Chile! I was extremely scared, not of the procedure but of what people would think of me after the surgery. Yes, I cared about what people thought about me because I had low self-esteem and was overweight with kids and divorced. Yep, kids. Did y'all read the part about not being scared of the procedure? Yep, I questioned that thought as well, but it was—what it was.

I was excited and pleased with the results of the procedure, though still embarrassed. I made my mom, you know my ride or die, promise not to tell anyone; not even my dad or Nikki ('cause she knows everything). Can you imagine asking that of your mom? I was at a low period in my life—'cause why did I place that much pressure on my mom. I eventually told my sisters and sister-cousin. They did not judge me at all—although you know that was the main reason why I wanted to keep it a secret—judgement. I am so grateful that I no longer carry that spirit with me.

So, keeping with the truth, when my close friends asked how I lost the weight, I lied. I gave them the regimen that I was given after surgery like it was a miracle drug. I am so embarrassed and ashamed. I couldn't tell the truth for those reasons. I was traumatized. I was always the chubby kid, friend, cousin, daughter. However, I was headed towards my skinny! Ha!

That was being honest. Promise. Dang. I guess that I needed to get that out!

Journal Entry

Write about your greatest obsession and how you overcame it. Let it out!

Chapter Six

Becoming Roni

I became Roni because I no longer liked who Ronda was. This may be hard for some to understand but it will make sense to others. When you stop liking who you are as a person, it is hard to look at yourself in the mirror each day. So, I changed my identity. I became Roni. A fun-loving serial dater that no longer gave a damn about what people thought about her. Roni is carefree and unapologetically. No one in my family understood when people started calling me Roni. It was like a foreign language to them. My kids were confused, but I couldn't explain it to them. Everyone just went with the flow of my newly found identity.

I never realized how much a name would impact your life. I loved becoming Roni. I was able to mask the hurt and pain that Ronda was in for years. I was able to do and hear things differently. I found that becoming Roni was my happy place, but also a facade. Was I being fake or becoming who I'd always wanted to be? The struggle is real, and I already told y'all that I am all over the place—but lock in.

I realize now that Roni and Ronda are the same people. Ronda was afraid, but Roni was fearless. Ronda was a people pleaser and Roni gives people the middle finger. Ha. Yep. Just like that. See, we always allow fear to change our lives over and over as a result of feeling as though we are not good enough, smart enough, haven't gone far enough, etc., We beat ourselves up or down and allow the opinion of others to trap our minds and play with our souls. Understand? Tuh. I know that sometimes it gets hard to come to realizations; recognizing that we were created uniquely, so we really don't have to become someone else. I just taught myself something. Stay with me.

Journal Entry

Have you ever felt lost?

Chapter Seven

Just Around Here —"Allowing"

There's that word allowing. I have learned that I was surviving not living while allowing shenanigans and foolishness into my life. I allowed myself to enter into relationships with men that weren't conducive to my needs or worth. I allowed myself to be there for people that were not there for me. I allowed foolishness in my life. Not intentionally; but I did allow it.

When you are out here surviving and not living, you allow so much. The survival piece is what we live by. For over twenty years, I allowed someone to play double dutch with my life. He would jump in, then jump out and I allowed him right back in. The toxicity was consistent and familiar.

Sometimes we have a false sense of reality, which to me—equates to being "just stupid." We already know what the end result will be because of history, but here we go—allowing the bullshit all over again. Didn't Auntie Maya say...

"When someone shows you who they are, believe them the first time."

We are just out here not listening to Auntie, who was a very wise woman. She also said, "People will forget what you said, people will forget what you did, but people will never forget how you made them feel." Whew! That is so real! So, what do we do — Ignore what we were taught, ignore the red flags, ignore all things and just keep allowing foolishness to happen.

I allowed one person to play with my time in a "double-dutch relationship." He literally jumped in and out of my life for over twenty years. Just foolish! Then I allowed a narcissist into my life. Whew! Big mistake. After reflecting over both "relationships," they taught me a valuable lesson. I AM ENOUGH!

Journal Entry

What have you allowed in your life that you know isn't right?

Chapter Eight

It's Always Your Own Kids

I don't know who told me to have kids. But they are here now and from my experience, will hurt you every chance that they get. I will never forget the six words that broke my heart into tiny pieces, literally. "I didn't ask to be born." Those words live rent free in my head. It felt like six knives being thrown directly at my heart. Bullseye. Pain. Heartache. Speechless. Typing this is painful but it is a part of my healing. Our kids will never understand. Ever. They will never understand how it feels to carry a baby in your womb created by God. Perfect. Then having to give birth. Pushing and pushing and pushing. Crushing bones and tearing muscles. Being ripped apart. Until. Ensuring that the perfection pushed out has all ten fingers and ten toes. Breathing. Feeding. Nurturing. Caring. Providing. The intense pain of having the one that you gave life to look at you and say, "I didn't ask to be born," never goes away. The disrespect. The shock. The fear. This taught me a lesson. No matter what you do for your kids, you are always the bad guy in their story. You are blamed for everything and all things. Trauma.

As mothers we keep all emotions inside because we are natural protectors. That day, my entire world fell apart because the sacrifices that I made were all in vain at that very moment. I was numb. Our kids will never understand that as mothers, we make things happen that no other can. We make miracles happen. Seriously. For my own child to say those words to me so effortlessly without caution or remorse spoke volumes. Every emotion that I had; was lost. Never regained. I could barely breathe. However, I handled myself well. It was at that point that I realized how much—I didn't matter.

I continued to try to be the best parent that I could be. Our kids did not come with instructions and no one prepared me for parenthood. All I knew was that I had four kids that I needed to provide for at all costs. No excuses. So, I continued. I convinced myself that I was not hurt and that I needed to just move on. Nothing is ever good enough. It happened again. My child spoke to me in such a poor manner that I was completely taken aback and knew that the devil had them by the neck. At that time, I was trying to heal from two surgeries. My child didn't get their way, made poor choices and then... Bam! The disrespect. Hardcore, painful disrespect with no filter followed by the word, "bruh." I was in disbelief and literally in a state of shock. I started speaking to God and praying for them at that very moment. That disrespect hit differently. It was as cold as it gets followed by the fire pit of hell. Have you ever been there with your kids? I remember not being able to swallow and developing a knot in my gut. It was that bad. All because I said, "no," for the first time. I said no. Then, the devil presented himself and I was stabbed again. This time it wasn't knives but an ax, a very sharp ax. Unbearable. Sharp. Pain. It's always your own kids. Devastated. At that moment, I felt defeated because I was trying to heal physically and this kid didn't care. Defeated. Again.

I started questioning myself as a parent. A single parent. A divorced parent. A working parent. A miracle working parent. A parent. A parent that only wants the best for my kids. I wasn't strict. That could be the problem. I didn't discourage my kids or curse them out. But maybe...never mind. Seriously, being disrespected by your own child is a different type of pain.

It's funny how the parent is always the problem or the issue. No accountability held by the kids that exude disrespect like an AK 47. But, I took those bullets like Cleo in *Set it Off*. Then the audacity of them (the kids) to diagnose you with a mental illness. Emotionally detached. Unemotional. Bipolar. Any and all diagnoses that they have learned through TikTok and Instagram; followed by the allegations of not listening or understanding. Chile, you left me at the disrespect. When you are disrespectful and consistent with the behavior, you receive nothing from me. Not even emotion. Kids want to play the adult role so badly and can't take it when you treat them the way they asked to be treated. Now, we become unemotional and distant because we demand respect from those that we take care of daily. Read that again.

I've mastered many things in my life—most importantly, I have mastered not allowing my children to break me. I allowed that for so many years—no more.

Journal Entry

How did you heal, from a time when your child/family member hurt you?

Chapter Nine

The Professional Chick

I'm just going to say this and say it loud. Being professional is so overrated and annoying. Just ghetto. Yep, I said "ghetto." What is professionalism, really. Everyone walks around with their own definition.

Well, here's mine.

Professionalism is a way for people to take advantage of your character and person. Think about it. In my profession, I get disrespected all day long by those in leadership positions. Society says that I am to be respectful of figures in positions higher than mine and I should be the bigger person when I find myself in a conflict or "situation." Is this really the truth? So, I have to subject myself to ignorance because society says that it is unprofessional if I respond? Oh, let's not forget that as a black woman if I respond in any way, I am called aggressive when essentially—I AM really passionate. Ha!

Professionalism is just a cop out for those that don't want to be read. Some of y'all will get that later. Seriously, why is it that when we want to speak up for ourselves, it's aggression? Think about it. One definition is having the competence or skill expected of a professional. Could I not be competent or skilled enough to tell you about yourself? That is professionalism defined, RIGHT? Whew! My professionalism is always tested!

Coming from a family of educators, I grew up strongly stating that I would never go into the field of education. Throughout my teenage years, I witnessed my mom, a head start educator, gather every child in our neighborhood and tutor them in reading. She was a Parent as Teacher volunteer and the "Educational Mother" of our Kirkwood suburbia neighborhood. My mom, along with her friends in Kirkwood/Meacham Park, provided educational opportunities for the neighborhood. As I observed their passion and became proud of their accomplishments, It piqued my interest in teaching our neighborhood kids to be successful and productive.

At the age of 15, I was hired as a camp counselor at Sprong Inc., a summer program developed to provide activities and academia to the children of the Kirkwood/Meacham Park area. This is where I found relationship building to be important when creating experiences for children. When you show children that you genuinely care, the process of learning begins; and their creative exploratory minds take them on academic journeys everywhere!

After my tenure in the Houston Independent School District, I moved back home to St. Louis. In the summer of 2010 I met Lynett Hookfin; a feisty, knowledgeable, intellectual, and dynamic Administrator. She became the principal of Normandy MS taking me under her wing as her first instructional coach/coordinator and then her Assistant Principal, to teach me, mold me and provide me with immediate feedback. This is when I learned the importance of leadership and confidence!

It was at Normandy Middle School, under the leadership of Dr. Hookfin, where I began to realize the significance of understanding student behaviors and dissecting the lives of our future as they traveled through hallways that were foreign to them. We needed to touch lives before attempting to teach academic lessons. And once their lives were touched, we witnessed academic excellence and success! I fell in love. I fell in love with the possibilities that are endless for our "babies"...our **B**old, **A**udacious, **B**eautiful, **I**ntelligent and **E**ver-Changing **S**tudents.

Dr. Hookfin helped me to realize my greatest potential, and when challenges gut punched me, she required that I "get myself together" and reminded me that I was built for the field of education ~ "my gift" is touching the lives of our future and ensuring that their academic needs are met—always. Dr. Hookfin became my mentor, pushing and challenging me in various capacities; and then my friend who surprised me with her presence as I received my Doctorate Degree in 2015. She is intriguing and I paid close attention! Her leadership and undying care for the academic success of all students molded me into the leader that I am today. Dr. Hookfin taught me how to be "softly direct" while articulating my needs as a leader and the needs of students to those that sometimes half-listen. The impact that Dr. Hookfin made on my life will be forever embedded.

When Dr. Hookfin journeyed into another position outside of Missouri, I had the pleasure of meeting Dr. Genita Williams as she would become the principal of Normandy Middle School. She, too, poured into my life;

teaching me leadership skills and providing feedback to ensure my success as an Administrator.

After reading articles about Dr. Howard Fields and his great work in the Riverview Gardens School District, he too was quite impactful, and he didn't know me at all. I followed him from Riverview to Webster Groves, then to Kirkwood, stoked by his ideas of Equity and Education and intrigued by his leadership. He was Dr. Hookfin and Dr. Williams combined with a twist. I eventually reached out to him and asked him to mentor me, offer feedback and provide a listening ear when I needed one. Without hesitation, Dr. Fields agreed—again, not knowing me at all. I share this because I would like people to know that it takes a village with educators as well. You never know who is watching, listening, notetaking and evaluating your work to become better versions of themselves. I could not be the leader that I am today without the aforementioned individuals and their leadership. It takes more than a degree and certification to be great at your career choice, it takes commitment, passion, dedication, and risk taking. As an Instructional Leader, I must be prepared to take risks to ensure the academic success of all students' post-secondary. Just call me a risk taker! My motivation for student success runs deep!

Journal Entry

Has your Professionalism been tested?

Chapter Ten

The Unstoppable Chick

In her song Unstoppable, Koryn Hawthorne said:

"They told you that you couldn't do it 'cause you're washed up
Ain't like them bad girls, said you should get your sauce up
But I got this plan and you might not understand
I'ma go hard as I can, and I'm gon' be the boss of it
Just watch me do this, put no limits only swagger on it
Walk right up to the front where I belong and brag on it
Go to the top, I'ma give it all I got
Might take a lot but we ain't gon' ever stop
I do believe I'm something special
Can't take that from me
So you can say what you want and I go harder, stronger
Be who I'm supposed to be
'Cause I'm unstoppable, I get all the way in it
That's the way I was made and I'm up on my business
'Cause I'm unstoppable, ain't no hoping and wishing
Say a prayer, catch your wave, then I go out and get it
'Cause I can be what I want, try it if I want
I'm powered by the King and He won't let me fall
'Cause I'm unstoppable, nah, nah, nah, He won't let me fall
No, no, no, no, no, 'cause I'm unstoppable"

I felt this in my soul and heart. I am unstoppable.

But then I got gut punched. Because. What is "unstoppable?" I was hyped and stuff until I started thinking like...girl...you have been writing this book for ten years talking about some "unstoppable." I'm cracking up because that is literally what I said to myself out loud, y'all. For real.

So, after being reflective; very reflective, I am unstoppable. In reality, I haven't missed a beat. I have learned to dance to the beat that is in my head and the lyrics that I choose at that moment. I keep going. Pushing. Crawling. Walking. Running. Sometimes even sprinting. And that is the definition of unstoppable. Going hard when you feel weak. Feeling weak but making it look strong. Feeling strong but mentally weak. Mentally weak but reflective. And the cycle continues. Some of you can relate. Especially if you are in the field of education.

Now, I know someone reading this will say, "Chile you need therapy." Been there and done that! Therapy didn't help me; however, you try it at your own pace. At one point, I was giving therapy when I was supposed to be getting therapy. Let that sink in.

Therapy is not for everyone; but healing is a factor in therapeutic practices for yourself. You'll get that as you continue to read. You must first understand what healing is and know that it is a process. Yes, a process. You first have to separate yourself from all things. Yep, that man, the kids, the selfish family members and opportunistic "friends."

Journal Entry

What makes you Unstoppable?

Chapter Eleven

The Praying Chick

Have you ever met someone who had the audacity? Let's first define the word because everyone doesn't know the correct meaning. I am laughing, but so serious. SO—defined by the Webster's Dictionary, the meaning of audacity is:

noun

- 1. A **willingness** to take bold risks.
- 2. Rude or **disrespectful** behavior; impudence.

So basically, people are around here volunteering their audacity and thinking that it is cute. It's not. Feelings get hurt. Mascara running. Nose snotting. Egos hurt. Then the grand entrance of the famous "Attitude." You hear the words, "She be tripping," uttered on a regular basis. This provoked prayer —because someone was about to get it. It went dark.

I remember being in a dark place when I asked God to teach me how to pray. I felt a little embarrassed because we all are supposed to know how to pray, right? That is the first thing that your family shouts when you are going through everything—Chile Pray!

Let me tell you about scripture. Scripture will have you rethinking your entire life. Scripture will hit you so hard that you would think a tsunami scooped you up. Look, Isaiah 43:2 says," *When you pass through the waters, I will be with you; and when you pass through the rivers they will not sweep over you. When you walk through the fire you will not be burned; the flames will not set you ablaze"* But wait... I kept reading and this jumped out:

The runt will become a great tribe, the weakling become a strong nation. I am God. At the right time, I'll make it happen. ~ Isaiah 60:22

Aww...ok! Read that again—if you choose to, 'cause baby when I tell you that scripture slapped me like Ike slapped Tina, I had to reimagine how my face looked; because Chile it was cracked. I was trying to do things my own way when I knew doggone well I needed to sit my butt down somewhere.

Anyway, look—I was experiencing every emotion and feeling as I was journeying through what I would describe as a taste of hell, also known as LIFE; scripture provoked my complete understanding of how to pray.

Watch this:

I was angry.

Ephesians 4:31

Ephesians 4:26

James 1:19

John 16:33

Saved me.

I worried myself sick.

Jeremiah 32:27

Saved me.

I was losing faith.

Hebrews 11:16

Saved me.

I was trying to figure it all out.

Joshua 1:9

Saved me.

I was confused while trying to understand my truth.

John 8:32

Saved me.

I started getting excited. Praying became my habit. Intentional praying became my habit. I BECAME. I AM.

I AM...

An overcomer

More than a conqueror

Joyful

Rich

Forgiven

Resilient

Powerful

Full of knowledge

Confident

Can you feel me getting bougie? I am not done. Hold on. BECAUSE. I AM...

Above and NOT beneath

The head and NOT the tail

I AM — Deuteronomy 31:8 and Romans 8:31. I AM experiencing God's goodness; Psalms 129:2 and I AM experiencing God's favor; Psalms 44:3 and I AM experiencing and understanding Peace; Phillipians 4:6; Exodus 14:14 to top it off with Isaiah 49:25.

Tuh! If y'all didn't get excited after reading that — y'all are lame.

Journal Entry

What does prayer look like for you? Do you know how to pray? Scribe your favorite scripture.

Chapter Twelve

Dealing with Trauma

I was married to a narcissist. His mother sat me down when she visited us and gave me intentional and detailed information about her ex-husband, my ex's dad. She was really warning me. It was subtle, but so detailed that it scared me. She spoke about my ex-husband's childhood and gave me intimate details about his growth and development as well as his rebellious ways. She went into detail about her troubled marriage—I felt that she was low key warning me; as did Grandmama and Auntie.

Yes, but I still married him, with all the warnings and red flags—I married him. Then he became. He "became" because I didn't fully know him. He became arrogant. He became accusatory. He became lazy. He became street. He became unfocused. He became important to himself. He became excessive in his own admiration. He became entitled. He became manipulative. He became needy. He became disrespectful. He "became" all the characteristics of a narcissist. Narcissist. Narcissistic. Narcissism. He became jealous. I tried. Trying wasn't enough.

I often blamed myself for saying "yes." Then I blamed myself for staying. I was filled with guilt. My guilt came from a dark place. Guilt was followed by anxiety—because how did I get to this place? The place of "allowing" a person to interrupt my life with negativity and opportunistic ways. He was waiting for the next hustle but not necessarily making the best decisions about family. Late night hustles and early morning silence. That became my reality. It became noticeable, then no more. I was fed up with being the only one trying and being blamed for it. Then it got real.

I didn't know that I was dealing with the trauma of a broken marriage until I no longer slept and became numb. I was spoken to abrasively by the one person that I felt would understand. His mom. Then his sisters. I was in total disbelief. That was traumatic. The ringing of voices that condoned negative behaviors. The name calling and excuses being made when the signs were clear. He (my ex) exhibited the same behaviors that his mother stated about his father. He was his father. He was intentional about creating a space of blame and taking no accountability.

I never spoke a negative word to the kids about their father. I knew that when the time came, they would see for themselves. The lies. Broken promises. Placing blame. The narcissistic behaviors. The distrust. The lack of parenting. Again, the lies.

The time came. I didn't say a word but, "Your dad loves you." Of course there was more that I wanted to say, but they will eventually find out on their own. It was so much pain that I kept in. The pain of the grandmother who acknowledged my first born, suddenly cut her off with no explanation. The pain of everyone ignoring the abuse that my first born endured in the hands of "him." The secrets and unsolicited drama. The lies. The trauma of knowing. Knowing that his mom's truth was real. Knowing that I should have the first time. Knowing that his intentions were strategic as he lured my friends to his corner. Friends. They were not my friends. Imagine thinking that you had a friend but all the while, she was talking to "him" and plotting on you.

Journal Entry

What trauma have you faced that you knew from the beginning—it was not the best decision?

Chapter Thirteen

Who Told Me to be a Parent?

I am on an uncomfortable spiritual journey ~ but I still curse and drink 'cause remember Jesus turned water into wine? It was meant for me to continue my wine indulgence, after all, my son did go to a Catholic School once. And it's ok to curse a lil' bit. You know that Jesus was cursing up a storm when He was walking and sweating. No — y'all seriously, this journey is making me so uncomfortable — I feel like I put my tampon in wrong every day. I'm just walking around trying to pretend that my tampon ain't at an angle; that's pretty much how my life is going; but y'all know that God is intentional and makes no mistakes, that's why I know there's something great planned for me.

I'm learning so much about myself as I journey. I found out that when someone asks you who you are, you should know. It's crazy how we walk around like we know ourselves when in reality, we are lost—only knowing our name. So who is expecting us to parent? Let's not even mention co-parent. This shit is whack, and without instructions; so we all out here just freestyling our kids' lives one child at a time 'cause the only thing we know is how our parents parented us, right or wrong.

Just confused.

'Cause who told me to be a parent?

I was supposed to be the rich auntie sending gifts from my condo in Turks and Caicos. No seriously, we parent the best way that we know how. That's why self-care, self-help, brown girl therapy and drinking adult beverages are so important. Lol! No—for real, as parents we have to take the time to reflect, relate and release before we knock a teen or teen-ish out, huh? That teen-ish is the one that wants to be in the teens so badly; they feel like they've been twelve forever. You know the ones who place emphasis on the teen, thirteen, fourteen, etc. We need time to rejuvenate and remind ourselves that we once had a flat belly or kinda flat belly before we gave birth to our broke best friends and crumb snatchers. We convince ourselves that we won't snap if we don't feel cute and then cry like the kids did something to us. Just a mess.

All because who told us to have kids? For real? We must take care of our mind, body and soul before we chin check the first child that says something stupid.

Like... "Mama, can I use your credit card to go online for a chance to be able to buy a $400 pair of sneakers."

Ok, I was venting but someone can relate. I know that self-care is the new big thing, but it should have BEEN a thing! We must stop surviving and start living. We don't want to mistakenly teach our children how to survive, if we do that, they will never know how to live. This is what we are seeing now with our youth in today's world. The world of social media and immediate access to everything. Immediate gratification in the form of likes and hearts. Our children don't know how to be patient.

Lawd, who told me to be a parent?

You can even get your Amazon order the next day—so today's generation is having a challenge dealing with patience, especially in school. We must do a better job at being intentional about what we teach and how we are raising and parenting our babies, those are two separate things; raising a child and parenting a child. It took me many years to figure that out and it's not even rocket science. Parenting and raising kids is just hard, difficult, and a challenge, that's why we must stick together as parents, ask each other questions and learn from each other's experiences and bad ass kids. Just kidding. There are no bad kids. They are just misunderstood. Lol, ha!

Why is it that this generation of kids could be misunderstood but we were either bad kids, fast little girls, or mannish little boys. Y'all remember, don't play. Kids nowadays have it good, well at least my three youngest 'cause I gave all my parenting and energy to that first born when I was in my 20-30s. I'm too tired now. They are too vocal and want to talk and discuss only what they want. Now if you are my age, you know damn well you are not trying to hear all that. I'm too tired, call your sister or auntie. I started having kids too late. I'm tired. Neck and back hurting. That's why we need to take care of ourselves mommas! We are broken down.

'Cause who told me to be a parent.

Journal Entry

Who told me to be a parent?
Expound on that thought.

Chapter Fourteen

Can't Make This Up

What my siblings don't know is that my vision and mission in life was based upon them. When I left for college they were all young, so I made it my personal mission to make them proud of me and set a glowing example of how they could lead an amazing life. Whew, Chile, that was a lot of pressure on me.

So, I started my journey for them as I always did; starting a journey for someone else. At one point, I thought I had seven siblings. Well, that changed when I received a phone call from Big Poppa telling me that I had a brother named Antonio. Big Poppa is my daddy pronounced deddy! And no one bet not say a bad thing about MY Big Poppa because he is perfect. Yep! That's my deddy. So when he revealed to me that I had another sibling, I was excited; but of course I had questions because, why?

I remember the first time that I met my new brother, I fell in love. He was the darker version of our Grandfather Wallace. He had ole eyes and a smile that melted my entire heart. I knew that he was my brother because he was just as silly as all of us. The way he walked and carried himself, the way he spoke and his vivid personality all screamed Wallace — because we are flawless. Yep, I said it! It was as if we had known each other our entire lives. Then, he hugged me and made me feel safe. My brother made me feel safe at first sight. I needed that because I was entering a phase in my life that would turn into seven years of what I would describe as hell and heartbreak.

Stay with me, the journey is continuing. My siblings were my motivating factor for all things until the birth of my babies. I am the oldest of nine —minus two—so technically I am the oldest of seven. I had to let two go. My siblings became my reason. My reason for graduating high school. My reason for graduating college. My reason for attempting marriage. My reason for seeking a doctorate degree. My reason for being. Pressure at its finest. But check this out. They grow up and become their own individual people. They change, mature and develop into their own beings. Mine did. Some became unrecognizable — figuratively.

However, I continued my journey which was actually their journey. I accomplished everything that I set out to complete on behalf of my siblings. Four degrees and a certificate later, I was done. Or so I thought.

What I learned is that everyone does not understand your love for them. I set out to be an example for my siblings — but it ended up being a life lesson for me. You cannot pack your bags and go off on a journey for other people. Did you read how many times I said that my journey was for my siblings? I got gut punched when I figured out that the journey was not for them but really a lesson that got placed strategically in my life for ME! Yes, It took almost thirty years for me to figure out that I was being prepared for my purpose. God was preparing me. Mentally. Emotionally. Physically.

At some point I became detached from my own journey.

Journal Entry

Is your journey really for you?

Chapter Fifteen

Shower Cry

Today I cried in the shower. Unlike other times, it was a calm and subtle cry. It didn't feel painful, but it did hurt. I received some disturbing news from work, my middle daughter is wilding out, my oldest son is just doing his own thing, my luggage was lost, people are rude, the guy I met (with his fine ass) didn't call, my hotel room was cold, I was hungry and I got caught up in every emotion that I possess! I felt it all, literally. Then, suddenly—I couldn't cry anymore. The emotion was there; however, the tears weren't. The hurt left. Lloyd began playing from my speaker:

"I lost it all, my friends, my loved ones

But in life, there's always a chance to grow

From the struggle, from the pain, from the realness...

Had to find a new approach to an old dream

And it's not to take a shot at my old team

I just want you to see..."

Now Lloyd was talking to a woman, but these words were so relevant to how I was feeling at that moment. I was feeling like damn, I need a new approach. My dream is the same; but I have to change up my team. Tuh. Yep, that's what I heard myself say. I just want to see. Here's the healing — understanding that a new approach is needed. Not placing blame on anyone but holding myself accountable for my chance to grow. Whew! I had a whole sermon with myself.

The sermon was followed by reflection. At that moment, I realized that I had not allowed myself to grieve. I had experienced so many losses within the last seven years. I was being strong. Internalizing my feelings. Masking my emotions and building a sustainable wall brick by brick around my heart. That was the cry. It wasn't about any of that other stuff that I mentioned. It was solely about my experienced trauma that was bleeding so heavily that a bandage couldn't stop the bleeding. I ran right into the arms of the Lord!

Journal Entry

When was the last time you had a good shower cry? What was the cry about?

Chapter Sixteen

When You Are Not Good

What happens when you are not good. I'm not asking with the expectation of receiving an answer; but as a statement—deep, huh? It's okay to not be okay. What's not ok is allowing yourself to sit in that dungeon and not turn on any lights. There's no digging out the dungeon, just walk out when you are ready. When I say ready, I mean when you have dealt with the anxiety, the depression, the worry or whatever led you to that dungeon—and has it been dealt with on your own terms—here's where it gets deep.

People are so quick to tell you about yourself and what you need as you are going through pitfalls—they mean no harm—but everyone's advice is not the nourishment that's needed to feed (heal) your emotions, feelings, or your body. However, at times it's not about healing—but controlling the pitfalls that you go through.

I now control my anxiety. I will no longer allow it to control me. My method for control is reflecting on the situation and telling myself to calm down while practicing breathing techniques.

Journal Entry

**Do you know and/or admit when you're not good?
Have you identified triggers?**

Chapter Seventeen

The Other Side of Healing

I turned 50 years old and gave the entire United States of America and all those that reside in it, the middle finger, actually two middle fingers! I did not know how fed up I was until October 10, 2024 — the day yo girl walked right into HERSELF!

October 2024, my birthday trip to Jamaica was cancelled due to a hurricane. I was so disappointed and discouraged because I was ready to live it up on the beach with my girls. Plans changed. We ended up on an impromptu road trip to Chicago. This is where it gets interesting.

As I sat in the back seat of the SUV, I started to have anxiety. Now, I was panicking as well because I had never felt anxiety like that before. It felt different. It felt traumatic. It felt like someone was squeezing the breath out of me. It felt like what I would imagine death feels like when it's taking its time. Some of you will reflect on that later. Stay with me. I changed positions in the seat. I tried to take small breaths. I sat up straight arching my back like I was in physical therapy. I took deep breaths. In and out. In and out. I took my shoes off. I rolled my neck. I was attempting to bring myself out of whatever was happening. I did everything but speak. I was in a vehicle with three others and sat in silence as I went through what I now know—was a panic attack. Yes. I was just as confused as you are now. But your girl was having a full blown panic attack. What was the panic about? I couldn't even speak. No words would come out. And I just dealt with it. Just like I do with all things in my life. Just deal with it.

Journal Entry

What does healing look like to you?

Chapter Eighteen

The Heal With Me Commandments (Tips)

Know Your Worth: Understand that you were created with intention.

Never Settle: Once you understand your worth you become unwilling to settle for foolishness or accept any level of disrespect or things that violates your boundaries.

Control Your Emotions: It's ok to be emotional—it is not ok to allow yourself to be stuck in an emotional rut. Allow yourself to feel. Do not give yourself permission to wallow.

Love who you are with intention, even if it makes others uncomfortable. Don't ever apologize for being YOU. 'Cause who gon' check you?

Want it more than you fear it. Go into it with fear but don't allow yourself to be fearful. Read that again. Just do it and do it scared—But don't be scary.

Give yourself a start. And start over as many times as needed. Madame CJ Walker stated, "I got my start by giving myself a start." 'Cause who is going to question you? Bye boo!

Remember that life is not a competition. Who cares what the next person has. 'Cause they may have caught a case. Tuh. Mind your own business and create a life that is conducive to your needs and allowances. Stop comparing and contrasting your life with others. They may be broken down and tired too. Ha!

Always be intentional! Reflect and dance on! Being intentional allows you to play by your own rules and dance to your own beat whether you can dance or not. Just for the record, I can dance.

Always be amusing! It does wonders for your soul. Coco Chanel said, "You live but once. You might as well be amusing."

Ladies, keep a tube of red lipstick at all times. Powerful.

Challenge yourself. Auntie Cissy, Cicely Tyson once stated that, "Challenges make you discover things about yourself that you never really knew." This helped me grow into not being fearful.

Always stand. Stand still. Keep your crown on. Don't let your chin fall.

I wasn't ready for half the shit that I have gone through, but clearly I am built for it! Tuh!

I am still standing.

I don't care who is not on my team anymore. I choose Me. I got shit to do.

Lastly, listen to trap/ratchet music daily and dance naked! Ha!

Journal Entry

Create your own heal with me commandments...
Ready, set, GO!

Chapter Nineteen

Turn Your Pain Into Purpose

Remember that word "purpose"? Well, I finally figured it out. My challenge is over. My purpose is to be resilient. I tell you what, I have been in pain literally and figuratively for years. My physical pain was unexplainable. The back pain. The neck pain. The shoulder pain. The arm pain. The leg pain. The hip pain. The face pain. The head pain. The doctor and specialists were unable to identify the source of the physical pain.

Then came that other pain. The pain of losing both grandmothers. The pain of disrespectful kids. The pain of losing my step-dad. The pain of being in another narcissistic relationship. The pain of losing myself. The pain of my son moving to another state. The pain of losing myself. The pain of a sick mother. The pain of losing close family relationships. The pain of losing myself. The pain of moving back to St. Louis. The pain. Period.

So they, yep they... diagnosed me with stress related pain. YES, that was the diagnosis. The neck. The back. The leg. The hip. The face. The self. All stress related pain. So, after I called off my engagement, I became unapologetically focused on myself. Fully. I am no longer Roni, I am Ronda. I AM Ronda Leah Wallace, a beautiful force that was born to conquer the entire world. That is it. That's the sentence. I literally looked in the mirror and said, "You better get it together." I had lost myself. I lost myself while finding those around me. That will make sense to my resilient folk!

Journal Entry

Are you ready to turn your pain into purpose?

Chapter Twenty

Finally... I Have Arrived!

The most important lesson that I have learned about life is that people really don't care. They don't care about listening to you because they are already thinking about their return verbal attack — even when the conversation is positive. I've learned that everyone doesn't care like you care. I've learned that it is very important to not take things personally and to be careful with my tongue. I've learned that everyone doesn't love like I love and can't communicate the way that I communicate. None of which I take personally.

I've learned to be unapologetically myself and to give the middle finger to those that are unkind. I've learned that the person that I have become; is amazing just as I am. I've learned that being alone is not an uncomfortable tragedy but a valuable and peaceful part of life. I've learned that being silent provokes self-esteem. I've learned the true meaning of friendships — everyone is not your friend and that is ok. I've learned to dress up whenever I want to — 'cause who gon' check me boo? Ha!

I've learned that God makes no mistakes. I've learned that you have to love your family from afar when they don't bring you peace. I've learned that dealing with grief is a life-long challenge — and grieving is ok. I've learned not to allow people to write the story of MY life — I own my own life. I've learned that everyone does not deserve an apology — it is ok to move on and remove people from your life that don't bring you joy. I've learned the true meaning of joy. I've learned to celebrate myself even when I am feeling defeated. I've learned that feeling defeated is ok, as long as you don't sit in that defeat.

I've learned that love is a four letter word with many definitions. I've learned not to give everyone grace — some don't deserve it — and that's ok. I've learned that as I navigate through life, I don't have to conform or fit in — I am a gem! It's ok to stand out. I've learned that everyone was not raised — some were born to only survive and not live. That's another book. I've learned to stop expecting ME from others — we are not the same. I've learned that the power of prayer is just that — powerful. I've learned not to put myself in positions to listen to people talk poorly about others. It's rather disgusting to judge when your skeletons are detrimental to everyone's health. Y'all will get that later. I've learned that depression is real; and you have to be intentional about not running into that deep place to hide. It's a cop out. I've learned that people need compliments — seriously — it's a part of their growth and development as a person. Reflect on that. I've learned that sitting by the swimming pool in a different country is needed. I've learned that traveling soothes the soul and creates happiness. I've learned that working "hard" and not smart will burn you out so fast — and no one cares. I've learned that people will always have something to say about you — and that's ok. I've learned that red lipstick is the key to happiness. For real!

I've learned that the devil is real; and he tries to take you down. I've learned that MY GOD is the realest and will lift you up every time! I've learned that caring about your physical health is mandatory if you want to live. Read that again. I've learned that no matter how much we want them to be smart, men are just dumb when it comes to relationships. Let's argue. I've learned that a relationship is not needed to fulfill your life. We can do bad by ourselves — real talk.

I've learned that deceitful people need hugs. I've learned to march to the beat of my own music and sing off key as much as I want — 'cause who is going to tell me to stop? I've learned that parenting is ghetto! Yes, ghetto and challenging. I've learned that I have done the best that I could and given it all that I had with raising four kids as a single parent — deal with that shit! I've learned that listening to ratchet music gives you another aspect of life. Just listen. I've learned that peace will not bring you happiness — happiness comes from within when you are fully connected with who you are as a person. I've learned that crying is a part of the healing process. Crying became my art. Another book. I've learned that fresh flowers provoke happiness — especially sunflowers. I've learned that you can't help everyone — every person is not helpable — seriously. I've learned not to allow anyone to play in my face. Personally or professionally — whatever that is.

I've learned to:

Always keep fresh flowers in the house.

Keep your favorite bottle of champagne on stand-by.

Keep a facial regimen.

Keep your favorite candle on stand-by.

Keep your favorite perfume and fragrances that you love.

Keep several pairs of house slippers that are classy and comfy.

Keep affirming yourself — 'cause on my momma I look good!

Keep cute pajamas — comfy cute ones — sexy ones — you may never know what your evening may bring! Ha!

Keep diamonds on deck!

Always remembers Kash's Kommandments! But most importantly, heal with me.

Ladies and gentlemen... I have arrived!

About the Author

Dr. Ronda Wallace has 28 years of educational experience at all levels. Currently, she serves as the Principal of Sumner High School, the first black high school west of the Mississippi River. Dr. Wallace earned a Bachelor of Arts degree in Psychology from Texas Southern University, a Master of Arts degree in Counseling from Prairie View A&M University, an Educational Specialist degree in Administration and a Doctor of Education Degree in Educational Administration from Lindenwood University. She is currently working on her Human Resources Certification.

Previously, Dr. Wallace has served as Principal of North Technical High School, Assistant Principal at Normandy Middle School and in many educational and leadership capacities within the Houston Independent School District in Houston, TX.

She has also taught grades 1-8 with a specialty in English and Writing and taught high school students during many summers. Dr. Wallace served as lead teacher and Teacher of the Year throughout her years in education. She is also a 2020 recipient of the Titus 2 Foundation Educator Impact Award, 2020 recipient of The St. Louis American Salute to Excellence Award, 2013 recipient of the Apple for The Teacher Award presented by Iota Phi Lambda Sorority, Incorporated Alpha Zeta Chapter, 2025 recipient of the Delux Power 100 and a member of Delta Sigma Theta Sorority Incorporated.

Dr. Wallace, whose educational philosophy is: Give them the opportunity, show them that you care, follow up and watch our future thrive in all capacities; has four children, Kharynton, Toni, and twin sons Langston and Landen.

Dr. Wallace is the founder and CEO of PrincipalChick Mentoring and Consulting, LLC.

www.ingramcontent.com/pod-product-compliance
Ingram Content Group UK Ltd.
Pitfield, Milton Keynes, MK11 3LW, UK
UKHW061954290726
14090UKWH00021B/1222